A Straightforward Guide to Letting Prop

LONDON BOROUGH OF HARROW
WITHDRAWN FROM STOCK
AND APPROVED FOR SALE
SOLD AS SEEN
PRICE: 50p

CONTENTS

Introduction

LETTING PROPERTY FOR PROFIT

This book is the first in a series of Straightforward Guides to property management. Its aim is to demonstrate in a clear and uncomplicated way the key elements in managing residential property for a profit.

Private lettings of residential property has grown significantly in the last ten years, particularly with the passage of the 1988 Housing Act, which gave landlords more incentive to let. However, sadly, those who are involved in letting property do not have the professional knowledge needed to manage effectively and often end up in a mess. Little thought is given to the fact that landlord and a complex framework of law, which both parties should recognize, covers tenant, the relationship between the two.

Whilst the public sector has taken great pains to educate the tenant, the private sector has not followed suit. This book should, hopefully, remedy some of those shortcomings and make the process of managing property for a profit that much easier.

Generally, the key to understanding any situation is having knowledge of a particular subject. The law relating to housing is one very important area.

This Straightforward Guide is intended to provide clear answers for the landlord, existing or potential by outlining the legal position and also rights and obligations in general, and by pointing to the way forward in a particular situation.

In addition, the guide should also be of use to the student who wants a brief introduction to the law relating to private residential lettings.

Each Chapter has a *key point's* section at the end, which summarizes the most important points raised in that particular chapter.

The guide deals with the status (position) of the landlord and tenant in law. It does so by guiding the reader briefly through the legal framework and highlighting the various types of tenancy agreements and the different areas of law under which they fall. It also deals more specifically with different tenure types and general rights and obligations concerning rent and repairs plus how to end the tenancy.

In addition, the position of the landlord and income tax, also housing benefit is covered, plus letting out rooms in ones own home and there is a section on how to recover the tenancy in court.

Overall, this guide should prove invaluable to those who are about to embark upon becoming a landlord for the first time, or those who are already landlords. It should also be useful for those who wish to study the area generally.

1

CONSIDERATIONS WHEN LETTING A PROPERTY

THE IMPORTANCE OF HAVING A CLEAR BUSINESS PLAN

Letting residential property for profit has become more and more common in the last ten years, particularly since the passage of the 1988 Housing Act, which gave potential landlords more incentive to let, by removing rent controls for property let after 1988 and also changing the tenancy in use to the assured tenancy, a version of which is the assured shorthold, fixed for a minimum period of six months and easily ended after that period.

Added to the passage of the 1988 Act has been the activities of the housing market, which boomed and then, predictably, went bust, leaving many in a state of negative equity. The more attractive option for many was to hold on to these properties until the housing market recovered and let them out to cover costs and to achieve a modest return on their investment.

In addition to the many who let property out of necessity and who are not "professional landlords" so to speak there are those who have built a business through acquiring properties, mostly through mortgage, and letting them out for a profit. These professional landlords differ as to their expertise, some being very unprofessional in their actual approach, having no idea of Landlord and Tenant law and no idea of the property world and subsequently very little idea of management. Often these people come unstuck and cause grief to others, whether intentionally or otherwise.

The aim of this brief book is to introduce the landlord, whether potential or already involved in the business, whether professional or merely nursing property through the recession, to the key aspects of the world of residential letting, in the hope that that person becomes more knowledgeable and that profit is maximised whilst management is effective and equitable.

What kind of property is suitable for letting?

Obviously, there are a number of different *markets* when it comes to people who rent. There are those who are less affluent, young and single, in need of a sharing situation, but more likely to require more intensive management than older more mature perhaps professional people who can afford a higher rent but require more for their money. The type of property you have, its location, its condition, will very much determine the rent levels that you can charge and the clients that you will attract.

The type of rent that a landlord might expect to achieve will be around ten per cent of the value of the freehold of the property, (or long leasehold in the case of flats). The eventual profit will be determined by the level of any existing mortgage and other outgoings. If you are renting a flat it could be that it is in a mansion block or other flatted block and the service charge will need to be added to the rent. When letting a property for a profit it is necessary to consider profit after mortgage payments and likely tax bill plus other outgoings such as insurance and agents fees (if any). Of course there are other factors which make the profit achieved less important, that is the capital growth of the property.

It is important to remember that, as a landlord letting property, there will not be the entitlement to MIRAS which a residential owner occupier would have. This will push up the cost.

THE BUSINESS PLAN

As a private landlord, a person considering letting a property for profit, or already doing so, it is vital that you are very clear about the following:

- What kind of approach do you intend to take as a landlord? Do you intend to purchase, or do you have, an upmarket property which you are going to rent out to stable professional tenants who will pay their rent on time and look after the property (hopefully!).

- What are the key factors that affect the value of a property in rental terms? Is the property close to public transport, does it have a garden, what floor is it on and what size are the rooms? Is it secure and in a crime free area. If you are acquiring a property you should set out what it is you are trying to achieve in terms of the longer term, i.e., the type of person you want and match this to the likely residential requirements of that hypothetical person. You can then gain an idea of what type of property you are looking for, in what area, and you can then see whether or not you can afford such a property. If not, you may have to change your plan.

- Do you intend to let to young single people, perhaps students, who will occupy individual rooms, achieving higher returns but causing potentially greater headaches? Are you aware of the headaches. It is vitally important that you understand the ramifications of letting to different client groups and the potential problems in the future.

- Are you clear about the impact on the environment, and to other people that your activities as a landlord may have? For example, do you have a maintenance plan which ensures that not only does your property look nice, and remain well maintained, will your maintenance plan, or a lack of it, impact on the rest of the neighborhood? Will the type of tenant you intend to attract affect the rest of those living in the immediate vicinity?

What are the aims and objectives underpinning your business plan? Do you have a business plan or are you operating in an unstructured way? Taking into account the above, it is obviously necessary that you have a clear picture of the business environment that you intend to operate in, the legal and economic framework that governs and regulates the environment.

It is vital that you are very clear about what it is you are trying to achieve. You should either understand the type of property that you already own or have an idea of the property you are trying to acquire to fit what client group. These goals should be very clear in your own mind and based on a long term projection, underpinned by a knowledge of the law and economics of letting property for a profit.

As an exercise you should sit down and map out your business plan, before you go any further. Whether you are an existing property owner, or wish to acquire a property for the purpose of letting, the first objective is to formulate a business plan.

2

FINDING A TENANT

Having laid out your business plan, based on the considerations outlined in chapter one, it is now necessary to look at the possible sources of tenant for your property. Remember, the tenant is the key to your future income and profit and also to your own personal peace or otherwise and therefore must be chosen extremely carefully. On the basis of your business plan you will know the type of person that you are prepared to accept because you will have identified what type of management scenario you wish. You will know their position, i.e., whether professional, student, working or on benefits or retired. In order to locate this person you will need to know the various sources available to you.

Letting Agents

There are obvious advantages in using an agent: they are likely to have tenants on their books; they are likely to be experienced and can vet tenants properly before signing a tenancy; they can provide you with a tenancy agreement and they can provide a service after the property is let. However, agent's charge for this service and their fees can vary enormously. It is up to you as a would be landlord to ensure you understand what it is they are charging and exactly what you are left with after the charges.

Some agencies will offer a guaranteed income for the duration of the contract that you have signed with them, even if a tenant leaves. However, you should be extremely careful here as a number of cases recently against such agencies have revealed that there are unscrupulous operators around.

If you do appoint an agent to manage a property you should agree at the outset, in writing, exactly what constitutes management. Failure to understand the deal between you and the agent can cost you dearly. For example, in a lot of cases, an agent will charge you a fixed fee, sometimes 1 months rental, for finding a tenant, but will then exercise the right that they have given themselves in the initial contract to sign a new agreement and charge another months rent after the tenancy has expired. In this way they will charge you a months rent every six months for doing nothing at all.

Agents will typically look after the following:

- Transfer the utility bills and the council tax into the name of the tenant.
- Arranging repairs to be done

- Paying for repairs, although an agent will only normally do this if rent is being paid directly to them and they can make appropriate deductions.

- Chase rent arrears

- Serve notices of intent to seek possession if the landlord instructs them to do. An agent cannot commence court proceedings except through a solicitor.

- Visit the property at regular intervals check that the tenants are not causing any damage.

- Dealing with neighbor complaints

- Banking rental receipts if the landlord is abroad

- Dealing with housing benefit departments if necessary.

The extent to which agents actually do any or all of the following really depends on the caliber of the agent. It also depends on the type of agreement you have with the agent. Like your initial business plan, you should be very clear about what it is you want from the agent and how much they charge.

Beware! There are many so-called rental agencies which have sprang up since the property recession and also the advent of "Buy to Let". These agents are not professional, do not know a thing about property management, are shady and should be avoided like the plague. Shop around and seek a reputable agent.

A typical management fee might be 10-15% of the rent, although, as stated, there are many ways of charging and you should be clear about this.
It is illegal for agencies to charge tenants for giving out a landlord's name and address. Most agencies will charge the landlord.

Advertisements

The classified advertisment section of local papers are good places to seek potential tenants, particularly if you wish to avoid agency charges. Local papers are obviously cheaper than the larger ones, such as the Evening Standard in London or the broadsheets such as the Guardian. The type of newspaper you advertise in will largely reflect what type of customer you are looking for. An advert in the pages of the Times would indicate that you are looking for a well-heeled professional and this would be reflected in the type of property that you have to let.

There are many free-ad papers and also you may want to go to student halls of residence or hospitals in order to attract a potential tenant. When you do advertise, you should indicate clearly the type of property, in what area, what is required, i.e., male or female only, and the rent. You should try and avoid abbreviations as this causes confusion.

The public sector

One other source of income is the local authority or housing association. Quite often, your property will be taken off your hands under a five year contract and you will receive a rental income paid direct for this period, with agreed increases. However, the local authority or housing association will demand a high standard before taking the property off your hands and quite often the rent achieved will be lower than a comparable market rent, in return for full management and secure income. If you wish to try this avenue then you should contact your local authority or nearest large association.

Showing the property to the tenant

Once you receive a response to your advertisement the next stage is to make arrangements for viewing the property. It is a good idea to make all appointments on the same day in order to avoid wasting time. If you decide on a likely tenant, it is wise to take up references, if you are not using an agency. This will normally be a previous landlord's reference and also a bank reference. Only when these have been received and you have established that the person(s) are safe should you go ahead. Make sure that no keys have been handed over until the cheque has been cleared and you are in receipt of a months rent and a months deposit.

FINDING A TENANT

Be strictly business like. You are letting property for a profit and the tenants are the key to that profit. A mistake at the outset can cost you dearly for a long time to come.

In chapter three we will explore the legal framework governing residential lettings.

3

THE LAW IN A NUTSHELL

EXPLAINING THE LAW

As a landlord or potential landlord it is very important to understand the rights and obligations of both yourself and your tenant, exactly what can and what cannot be done once the tenancy agreement has been signed and the tenant has moved into the property.

Some landlords think they can do exactly as they please, because the property belongs to them. Some tenants do not know any differently and therefore the landlord can, and often does, get away with breaking the law. However, if you are about to embark upon a career as a budding landlord, letting property for profit, then it is important that you have a grasp of the key principles of the law.

In order to fully understand the law we should begin by looking at the main types of relationship between people and their homes.

The freehold and the lease

In law, there are two main types of ownership and occupation of property. These are: freehold and leasehold. These arrangements are very old indeed.

Freehold

If a person owns their property outright (usually with a mortgage) then they are a freeholder.

The only claims to ownership over and above their own might be those of the building society or the bank which lent them the money to buy the place. They will re-possess the property if the mortgage payments are not kept up with.

In certain situations though, the local authority (council) for an area can affect a person's right to do what they please with their home even if they are a freeholder. This will occur when planning powers are exercised, for example, in order to prevent the carrying out of alterations without consent.

The local authority for your area has many powers and we will be referring to these regularly in each Chapter of this Guide.

Leasehold

If a person lives in a property owned by someone else and has a written agreement allowing them to occupy the flat or house for a period of time i.e., giving them permission to live in that property, then they will, in the main, have a lease and either be a leaseholder or a tenant of a landlord.

The main principle of a lease is that a person has been given permission by someone else to live in his or her property for a period of time. The person giving permission could be either the freeholder or another leaseholder.

The tenancy agreement is one type of lease. If you have issued a tenancy agreement then you will have given permission to a person live in your property for a period of time.

The position of the tenant

The tenant will usually have an agreement for a shorter period of time than the typical leaseholder. Whereas the leaseholder will, for example, have an agreement for ninety-nine years, the tenant will have an agreement, which either runs from week to week or month to month (periodic tenancy) or is for a fixed term, for example, one-year.

These arrangements are the most common types of agreement between the private landlord and tenant.

The agreement itself will state whether it is a fixed term or periodic tenancy. If an agreement has not been issued it will be assumed to be a periodic tenancy.

Both periodic and fixed term tenants will usually pay a sum of rent regularly to a landlord in return for permission to live in the property (more about rent and service charges later)

THE TENANCY AGREEMENT

The tenancy agreement is the usual arrangement under which one person will live in a property owned by another. Before a tenant moves into a property he/she will have to sign a tenancy agreement drawn up by a landlord or landlord's agent.

A tenancy agreement is a contract between landlord and tenant.

It is important to realize that when you sign a tenancy agreement, you have signed a contract with another person, which governs the way in which they will live in their property.

The contract

Typically, any tenancy agreement will show the name and address of the landlord and will state the names of the tenant(s).The type of tenancy agreement that is signed should be clearly indicated. This could be, for example, a Rent Act protected tenancy (Chapter Two), an assured tenancy (Chapter Three) or an assured shorthold tenancy (Chapter Three). In addition there are several other less common tenancy types in use also indicated in this book.

The date the tenancy began and the duration (fixed term or periodic) plus the amount of rent payable should be clearly shown, along with who is responsible for any other charges, such as water rates, council tax etc, and a description of the property you are renting out.

In addition to the rent that must be paid there should be a clear indication of when a rent increase can be expected. This information is sometimes shown in other conditions of tenancy, which should be given to the tenant when they move into their home. The conditions of tenancy will set out landlords and tenants rights and obligations.

If services are provided, i.e., if a service charge is payable, this should be indicated in the agreement.

The tenancy agreement should indicate clearly the address to which notices on the landlord can be served by the tenant, for example, because of repair problems or notice of leaving the property. The landlord has a legal requirement to indicate this.

The tenancy agreement will either be a basic document with the above information or will be more comprehensive. Either way, there will be a section beginning "the tenant agrees." Here the tenant will agree to move into the property, pay rent, use the property as an only home, not cause a nuisance to others, take responsibility for certain internal repairs, not sublet the property, i.e., create another tenancy, and various other things depending on the property.

There should also be another section "the landlord agrees". Here, the landlord is contracting with the tenant to allow quiet enjoyment of the property. The landlord's repairing responsibilities are also usually outlined.

Finally, there should be a section entitled "ending the tenancy" which will outline the ways in which landlord and tenant can end the agreement. It is in this section that the landlord should make reference to the "grounds for possession". Grounds for possession are circumstances where the landlord will apply to court for possession of his/her property. Some of these grounds relate to what is in the tenancy, i.e., the responsibility to pay rent and to not cause a nuisance.

Other grounds do not relate to the contents of the tenancy directly, but more to the law governing that particular tenancy. The grounds for possession are very important, as they are used in any court case brought against the tenant. Unfortunately, they are not always indicated in the tenancy agreement. As they are so important they are summarized in Chapters two and three dealing with different tenancy types.

It must be said at this point that many residential tenancies are Very light on landlord's responsibilities. Repairing responsibilities, and responsibilities relating to rental payment, are landlords obligations under law. This book deals with these, and other areas. However, many landlords will seek to use only the most basic document in order to conceal legal obligations.

The public sector tenancy (local authority or housing association), for example, is usually very clear and very comprehensive about the rights and obligations of landlord and tenant. Unfortunately, the private landlord often does not employ the same energy when it comes to educating and informing the tenant. This is one of the main reasons for this book. It is essential that those who intend to let property for profit are able to manage professionally and set high standards as a private landlord. This is because the sector has been beset by rogues in the past.

Appendix 1 shows what a typical residential tenancy agreement should look like.

The responsibility of the landlord to provide a tenant with a rent book

If the tenant is a weekly periodic tenant the landlord must provide him/her with a rent book and commits a criminal offence if he/she does not do so. This is outlined in the Landlord and Tenant Act 1985 sections 4 - 7. Under this Act any tenant can ask in writing the name and address of the landlord. The landlord must reply within twenty-one days of asking.

Overcrowding and the rules governing too many people living in the property

It is important to understand, when signing a tenancy agreement, that it is not permitted to allow the premises to become overcrowded, i.e., to allow more people than was originally intended, (which is outlined in the agreement) to live in the property! If a tenant does then the landlord can take action to evict.

Different types of tenancy agreement

The protected tenancy - the meaning of the term

As a basic guide, if a person is a private tenant and signed their current agreement with a landlord before 15th January 1989 then they will, in most cases, be a protected tenant with all the rights relating to protection of tenure, which are considerable. Protection is provided under the 1977 Rent Act.

The rights of the protected tenant are explained more fully in Chapter four. We will also discuss those tenancies, which are not protected, even though they were signed before 15th January 1989.

The assured tenancy - what it means

If the tenant entered into an agreement with a landlord after 15th January 1989 then they will, in most cases, be an assured tenant. There are various types of assured tenancy.

At this point it is important to understand that the main difference between the two types of tenancy, protected and assured, is that the tenant has less rights as a tenant under the assured tenancy. For example, they will not be entitled, as is a protected tenant, to a fair rent set by a Rent Officer.

In Chapters two and three we highlight the differences between the rights of protected and the rights of assured tenants.

OTHER TYPES OF AGREEMENT

In addition to the above tenancy agreements, there are other types of agreement sometimes used in privately rented property. One of these is the licence agreement. The person signing such an agreement is called a licensee.

Although we will be discussing other types of agreements in existence, It must be said that the main agreements in use are either the protected tenancy to a certain extent or, more commonly now, the assured tenancy and therefore we will not be devoting any more time to the licence.

THE SQUATTER (TRESPASSER)

In addition to the tenant and licensee, there is one other type of occupation of property, which needs mentioning. This is squatting.

The squatter is usually someone who has gained entry to a vacant property, either a house or a flat, without permission.

Although the squatter, a trespasser, has the protection of the law and cannot be evicted without a court order, if he or she is to be given the protection of the law, the squatted property must have been empty in the first place.

On gaining entry to a property, the squatter will normally put up a notice claiming squatter's rights which means that they are identifying themselves as a person or group having legal protection until a court order is obtained to evict them. Even if no notice is visible, the squatter has protection and it is an offence to attempt to remove them forcibly.

The squatter has protection from eviction under the Protection from Eviction Act 1977 and is also protected from violence or harassment by the Criminal Law Act of 1977.

The trespasser who has entered an occupied property without permission has fewer rights. Usually, the police will either arrest or escort a trespasser off the premises. There is no protection from eviction. However, there is protection from violence and intimidation under the Criminal Law Act of 1977.

CRIMINAL JUSTICE AND PUBLIC ORDER ACT 1994 SECTIONS 72 Ð 76

This Act does allow a landlord to use reasonable force if there is a displaced residential occupier, or someone who has come home to find a trespasser occupying his home. However, the use of reasonable force has not been defined. The above Act amends the Criminal Law Act 1977. Other Sections of the 1994 Act dealing with squatters have serious implications but are not yet law at the time of writing.

As it is the private tenant we are concerned with in this book, no further mention will be made of the squatter or trespasser.

Now read the Key Points from Chapter three.

Key Points

- **Private Tenant**. A tenant of a landlord who is not a public landlord, public landlord being for example a local authority or housing association. The most common private tenancy relationship is between two individuals or between an individual and a company.

- **Leasehold and freehold**. These are the two main types of ownership of land and occupation of property. A freeholder will own the property outright (usually with a mortgage). A leaseholder has the right to live there for a period of time.

- **Tenancy agreement**. The tenancy agreement is one form of lease. It is a contract between the landlord and tenant for the occupation of property. The tenancy agreement is either for a specific length (e.g., six months) of time or from week to week or month to month.

The agreement will govern the length of notice given by the landlord or tenant when requiring the property back, or, in the case of the tenant, leaving the property.

- **Rent book**. If a tenancy is a weekly periodic tenancy, then a landlord must provide a tenant with a rent book.

- **Overcrowding**. A tenant must not allow his/her home to become overcrowded. A landlord can take a tenant to court and can evict in this case.

- **The protected tenancy**. The usual agreement signed by the private landlord and his or her tenant, before 15th January 1989 was the protected tenancy, so called because of the considerable rights given to this type of tenant under the 1977 Rent Act. Chapter Two deals with the protected tenant in more depth.

- **The assured tenant**. This is the usual type of tenancy agreement

29

entered into after 15th January 1989, which is regulated by the 1988 Housing Act, which gives fewer rights than the protected tenancy. In Chapter Two we discuss this type of agreement.

- **The licence and the licensee**. This is one type of agreement between landlord and tenant, which gives the occupier fewer rights than a protected tenant. More about the licence in Chapter Two.

- **Other types of agreement**. There are other types of agreement, which are not assured or protected. These are discussed in Chapter Two.

- **The squatter (trespasser)**. The squatter is someone who has entered a vacant property without permission and set up home there. The squatter can be evicted only with a court order. However, someone who has entered an occupied property, has no protection at all and can be removed immediately by the police.

4

THE PROTECTED TENANT

THE PROTECTED TENANT AND RENT ACT PROTECTION

In Chapter three we talked briefly about the meaning of the protected tenancy.

We saw that if a tenancy agreement was granted before 15th January 1989 then, in most cases, it will be a Rent Act protected agreement. However, there are a number of exceptions to this and they are listed further on in this chapter.

Many tenancies nowadays are assured tenancies. However, despite this, there are a significant number of older Rent Act protected tenancies in existence.

What Rent Act protection means is that the rules, which guide the conduct of the landlord and tenant are laid down in the 1977 Rent Act.

This Act was passed to give tenants more security in their home. It is called a Rent Act because its main purpose is to regulate rents, but the Act also gives tenants other rights such as protection from eviction.

It is mainly only tenants who can enjoy protection under the Rent Act of 1977, not usually licensees or trespassers who have limited rights. A tenancy will be protected provided that the landlord does not live on the premises. If a landlord lives in the same accommodation as the tenant then the tenant will not be protected by the 1977 Rent Act. To live in the same premises means to share the same flat as the tenant and not, for example, to live in the same block of flats.

In addition, Rent Act protection means that the rent will be regulated . This basically means that the tenant has the right to a fair rent set by a Rent Officer employed by the local authority.

The fair rent is set every two years and the landlord is not free to charge as he or she wishes. Once set the rent cannot be altered.

Rent Act protection also means protection from eviction which means that the landlord is not free to evict. For a tenancy to be protected, however, the tenant must be using the property as his/her main residence. If they are not, and the fact can be proved, then they will lose protection and the landlord can evict with less trouble.

SECURITY: THE WAYS IN WHICH THE TENANT CAN LOSE HIS/HER HOME AS A PROTECTED TENANT

As we saw in Chapter three, when a tenancy agreement is signed a contract is formed where both landlord and tenant are agreeing to accept certain rights and responsibilities.

In the agreement, there are a number of grounds for possession, which enable the landlord to recover his or her property if the contract is broken by the tenant, e.g., by not paying the rent. These may not always be referred to in the agreement but this can be found in the 1977 Rent Act.

If a landlord wishes to take back his or her property he/she must serve the tenant with a notice to quit (the premises) which must give twenty eight days notice of intention to seek possession of the property (to begin to recover the property) and, following the expiry of the twenty eight days an application must be made to court to repossess the property.

Appendix 2 shows a typical Notice to Quit, in the form in which a landlord must serve it.

When the landlord serves the notice to quit the reasons for his doing so should be stated in a covering letter to the tenant and should be based on the grounds for possession outlined in the agreement.

A landlord cannot simply evict a tenant, or use menaces (harassment) to do so. There is protection (Protection from Eviction Act 1977) and the landlord must apply to court to get a tenant out once the twenty-eight days have expired.

When a landlord has served a notice to quit, a tenancy becomes a "statutory tenancy" which exists until a court order brings it to an end.

Briefly, the reasons for a landlord wanting possession will be based on one of ten mandatory or ten discretionary grounds for possession.

Mandatory grounds for possession means that the court must give the landlord possession of the property, which means that the judge has no choice in the matter.

Discretionary grounds for possession means that the court can exercise some discretion in the matter (i.e., can decide whether or not to order eviction) and it is up to the landlord to prove that he is being reasonable. Discretionary grounds usually correspond to the tenant's obligations in the tenancy.

It is very rare, in the first instance, if the grounds are discretionary, for a landlord to gain possession of a property unless it is obviously abandoned or the circumstances are so dramatic. Usually a suspended order will be granted.

A suspended order means that the tenant will be given a period of time within which to solve the problem, i.e., come to an agreement with the landlord. This time period is, normally, twenty-eight days. So, for example, if a tenant has broken an agreement to pay the rent, the judge may give twenty-eight days in which either to pay the full amount or to reach an agreement with the landlord.

Listed below are the grounds for possession, which can be used against a tenant by a landlord. Full details of all grounds can be found in the 1977 Rent Act, which can be found in a local library.

Remember that these grounds are for *protected* tenants only.

The discretionary grounds for possession of property

Ground One is where the tenant has not paid his or her rent or has broken some other condition of the tenancy.

Ground One covers any other condition of the tenancy. This includes noise nuisance, unreasonable behavior and, usually, racial or sexual harassment.

Ground Two is where the tenant is using the premises for immoral or illegal purposes, e.g., selling drugs, prostitution. It also covers nuisance and annoyance to neighbors.

Grounds Three and Four are connected with deterioration of the premises as a direct result of misuse by the tenant.

Ground Five is that the landlord has arranged to sell or let the property because the tenant gave notice that he was giving up the tenancy.

Ground Six arises when the tenant has sub-let the premises, i.e., has created another tenancy and is no longer the only tenant. Usually, the landlord will prohibit any sub-letting of a flat.

Ground Seven no longer exists.

Ground Eight is that the tenant was an employee of the landlord and the landlord requires the property for a new employee.

Ground Nine is where the landlord needs the property for himself or certain members of his family to live in.

Ground Ten is that a tenant has charged a subtenant more than the Rent Act permits.

One other important discretionary ground does not appear in the list of grounds in the 1977 Rent Act. It relates to the provision of suitable alternative accommodation. If the landlord requires possession of the property for reasons such as carrying out building works then it must be demonstrated that suitable alternative accommodation can be provided by the landlord for the tenant.

The mandatory grounds for possession of a property occupied by a protected tenant

These are grounds on which the court must give possession of a property to the landlord. The judge has no choice in the matter. If such an order is granted then it cannot be postponed for more than fourteen days, except where it would cause exceptional hardship when the maximum is six weeks. There are two basic rules for using the mandatory grounds:

1. The landlord must give a written notice saying that he/she may in future apply for possession under the appropriate ground. He/she must give it to the tenant normally when or before the tenancy begins (before the tenancy was granted, in the case of shorthold) and;

2. When he/she needs possession, the conditions of the appropriate ground must be met.

The mandatory grounds are as follows:

Ground Eleven. This ground is available only when the landlord has served notice at the beginning of the tenancy stating when he or she wants back the premises, i.e., a date is specified.

Ground Twelve is valid only when a landlord has served notice that the property may be required for personal use as a retirement home.

Ground Thirteen applies only where the letting is for a fixed term of not more than eight months and it can be proved that the property was used as a holiday letting for twelve months before the letting began.

Ground Fourteen is that the accommodation was let for a fixed term of a year or less, having been let to students by a specified educational institution or body at some time during the previous twelve months.

Ground Fifteen is that the accommodation was intended for a clergyman and has been let temporarily to an ordinary client.

Ground Sixteen is that the accommodation was occupied by a farm worker and has been let temporarily to an ordinary tenant.

PRIVATE SECTOR AGREEMENTS SIGNED BEFORE JANUARY 1989 BUT WHICH DO NOT HAVE RENT ACT PROTECTION:

Not all people who entered into agreements before 15th January 1989 will be protected tenants under the 1977 Rent Act.

Agreements signed before 1989, which are not protected

There are certain types of agreement, which will not be classed as a protected tenancy.

Tenancies granted before 14th August 1974, and which are furnished with a resident landlord

If a tenancy was entered into before the above date and the property was furnished to a reasonable standard it is not considered to be protected. This is another complex area and will not be pursued further here.

Restricted contracts under the 1977 Rent Act

A tenancy entered into before 15th January 1989 will not be protected if, when the tenancy was first entered into, the landlord was still living in the same building as the property, which has been let to the tenant. This is known as a restricted contract. The exception is the situation where the block is purpose-built and the landlord has a separate flat.

However, if one landlord sells his interest to another person who intends to live in the building, the tenancy will remain unprotected for twenty-eight days. In that twenty-eight days the person taking over the property can either take up residence or serve written notice that he intends to do so within the next six months.

As long as he/she takes up residence within six months the notice serves to prevent the tenancy becoming protected.

If a tenancy is not protected because it falls within the above category then it is known as a restricted contract. However, one important point is that a restricted contract will cease to be such after the passing of the 1988 Rent Act when there is a change in the amount of rent payable under the contract other than a change determined by the rent tribunal.

From then on, the restricted contract becomes an assured tenancy. More about assured tenancies later.

Flats and houses under certain ratable values

If the property has a ratable value of over £750 (£1,500 in Greater London) that property cannot be the subject of a protected tenancy. In practice, few properties are above this figure.

Even after the change from ratable values to community charge and the council tax in 1993, the ratable value of a property will still apply in this case.

Tenancies at low rents

A tenancy, which was entered into before 1st April 1990 is not a protected tenancy if the rent paid, is less than two-thirds of the ratable value of the property on the appropriate day. The appropriate day is 23rd March 1973 unless the property was valued at a later date. If no rent is paid then the tenancy will not be protected.

Flats and houses let with other land

If a property is let with other land to which it is only an adjunct (an addition) then it will not be a protected tenancy. However, importantly, unless the other land consists of more than two acres of agricultural land, it will be taken as part of the dwelling house and will not prevent the tenancy being protected.

Payments for board and attendance

If a part of the rent for which a house is let is payable in respect of board or attendance there will not be a protected tenancy.

Board, which is the provision of meals, must be more than minimal if the tenancy is not to be protected. Provision of a continental breakfast would be enough, whilst the provision of hot drinks would not.

Attendance includes personal services such as making beds. This provision is one that is often used by landlords to avoid the Rent Act. Such a tenancy, though, may form a restricted contract (see above).

Lettings to students

A tenancy granted by a specified educational institution to students studying will not be protected (the institution will usually be a university or college of further education).

Holiday lettings

A tenancy is not a protected tenancy if its purpose is to give the tenant the right to occupy the dwelling for a holiday.

Agricultural holdings

A tenancy is not protected if the dwelling is part of an agricultural holding and is occupied by the person responsible for the control of the farming of the holding. Tenancies of this sort are subject to the control of the Agricultural Holdings Act 1986 and other areas of the law.

Licensed premises

Where a tenancy of a dwelling house consists of or comprises premises licensed for the sales of alcohol, there will not be a protected tenancy.

Resident landlords

The tenancy will not be protected if, at the commencement of the tenancy, the landlord was resident in the same building as the property, which has been let. This does not apply if the landlord merely has another flat in a purpose-built block; he must be in the same building or residence.

Where the landlord is a local authority, the Crown, a housing association or a co-operative

The tenancy will not be protected where the landlord is one of the above. Tenants of local authorities, housing associations, the Crown or a Co-operative has a different sort of protection, which this guide does not go into.

Company lets

Only an individual person is capable of living in a flat or house. If a property is let to a company there can be no statutory (legal) tenancy. When a property is let to a company, the tenancy would be between that company and a landlord. There are certain circumstances, however, where a company let can be a protected tenancy and the fair rent legislation applies.

Now read the Key Points from Chapter four.

Key Points

- **Rent Act protection**. This means that the rules, which guide the conduct of the landlord and tenant are laid down in the 1977 Rent Act.

- **Protection**. Mainly only tenants can enjoy protection under the Rent Act, not usually licensees or trespassers who have limited rights.

- **Resident landlord**. A tenancy will be protected provided that the landlord does not live on the premises.

- **Rent**. If a tenancy is protected rent will be regulated.

- **Eviction**. If a landlord wants to evict a protected tenant he/she must give twenty-eight days notice, using one of the grounds for possession outlined in the tenancy agreement or in the 1977 Rent Act.

- **The Licence**. There are a number of agreements signed before 1st January 1989 that are not protected and provide less security. The licence is one such agreement.

- **Other agreements**. In addition to the licence, there are a number of other agreements, which do not have protection under the 1977 Rent Act.

5

ASSURED TENANTS

THE ASSURED TENANT

As we discussed in Chapter three, all tenancies, with the exceptions detailed entered into after 15th January 1989, are known as assured tenancies. Assured tenancies are governed by the 1988 Housing Act, as amended by the 1996 Housing Act. It is to these Acts, or outlines of the Acts that the landlord must refer when intending to sign a tenancy and let a residential property.

The normal contractual period of the assured tenancy will usually be from week to week or month to month. There can also be a fixed term assured tenancy, the assured shorthold, which we will be discussing later.

Assured tenancies are not protected as are most tenancies signed before 1989, do not have the right to a fair rent and do not have the same rights as protected tenancies.

For a tenancy to be assured, three conditions must be fulfilled:

1. The premises must be a dwelling house. This basically means any premises, which can be lived in. Business premises will normally fall outside this interpretation.

2. There must exist a particular relationship between landlord and tenant. In other words there must exist a tenancy agreement. For example, a licence to occupy, as in the case of students, or accommodation occupied as a result of work, cannot be seen as a tenancy. Following on from this, the accommodation must be let as a single unit. The tenant,

who must be an individual, must normally be able to sleep, cook and eat in the accommodation. Sharing of bathroom facilities will not prevent a tenancy being an assured tenancy but shared cooking or other facilities, such as a living room, will.

3. The third requirement for an assured tenancy is that the tenant must occupy the dwelling as his or her only or principal home. In situations involving joint tenants at least one of them must occupy.

Assured tenants can be evicted only on certain grounds (some discretionary, some mandatory, as with the protected tenancy);

In order for the landlord of an assured tenant to regain possession of the property, a notice of seeking possession (of property) must be served, giving fourteen days notice of expiry and stating the ground for possession. A copy of this notice is shown in Appendix 3. This notice is similar to a notice to quit, discussed in the previous chapter.

Following the fourteen days a court order must be obtained.

Fast track possession

In November 1993, following changes to the County Court Rules, a facility was introduced which enables landlords of tenants with assured and assured shorthold tenancies to apply for possession of their property without the usual time delay involved in waiting for a court date and attendance at court. This is known as "fast track possession" and can only be used for certain grounds, grounds 1,3,4,5 and for shorthold tenancies for recovery of property. It cannot be used for rent arrears or other grounds.

If the landlord wishes to raise rent, at least one month's minimum notice must be given. The rent cannot be raised more than once for the same tenant in one year. Tenants have the right to challenge a rent increase if they think it is unfair by referring the rent to a Rent Assessment Committee. The committee will prevent the landlord from raising the rent above the ordinary market rent for that type of property.

TENANCIES WHICH ARE NOT ASSURED

A tenancy agreement will not be assured if one of the following conditions applies:

The tenancy or the contract was entered into before 15th January 1989;

If no rent is payable or if only a low rent amounting to less than two thirds of the present ratable value of the property is payable.

If the premises are let for business purposes or for mixed residential and business purposes;

If part of the dwelling house is licensed for the sale of liquor for consumption on the premises. This does not include the publican who lets out a flat;

If the dwelling house is let with more than two acres of agricultural land;

If the dwelling house is part of an agricultural holding and is occupied in relation to carrying out work on the holding;

If the premises are let by a specified institution to students, i.e., halls of residence;

If the premises are let for the purpose of a holiday;

Where there is a resident landlord, e.g., in the case where the landlord has let one of his rooms but continues to live in the house;

If the landlord is the Crown (the monarchy) or a government department. Certain lettings by the Crown are capable of being assured, such as some lettings by the Crown Estate Commissioners;

If the landlord is a local authority, a fully mutual housing association (this is where you have to be a shareholder to be a tenant) a newly created Housing Action Trust or any similar body listed in the 1988 Housing Act.

If the letting is transitional such as a tenancy continuing in its original form until phased out, such as:

A protected tenancy under the 1977 Rent Act;

Secure tenancy granted before 1st January 1989, e.g., from a local authority or housing association. These tenancies are governed by the 1985 Housing Act).

SECURITY: THE WAYS IN WHICH A TENANT CAN LOSE THEIR HOME AS AN ASSURED TENANT-LANDLORD REGAINING POSSESSION

We saw with the protected tenancy how there are a number of circumstances called grounds (mandatory and discretionary) whereby A landlord can start a court action to evict a tenant. The same position applies to assured tenants.

The following are the *mandatory* grounds (where the judge must give the landlord possession) and *discretionary* grounds (where the judge does not have to give the landlord possession) on which a court can order possession if the home is subject to an assured tenancy.

The mandatory grounds for possession of a property let on an assured tenancy

There are eight mandatory grounds for possession, which, if proved, leave the court with no choice but to make an order for possession. It is very important that you understand these.

Ground One is used where the landlord has served a notice; no later than at the beginning of the tenancy, warning the tenant that this ground may be used against him/her.

This ground is used where the landlord wishes to recover the property as his or her principal (first and only) home or the spouse's (wife's or husbands) principal home. *The ground is not available to a person who bought the premises for gain (profit) whilst they were occupied.*

Ground Two is available where the property is subject to a mortgage and if the landlord does not pay the mortgage, could lose the home.

Grounds Three and Four relate to holiday lettings.

Ground Five is a special one, applicable to ministers of religion.

Ground Six relates to the demolition or reconstruction of the property.

Ground Seven applies if a tenant dies and in his will leaves the tenancy to someone else: but the landlord must start proceedings against the new tenant within a year of the death if he wants to evict the new tenant.

Ground Eight concerns rent arrears. This ground applies if, both at the date of the serving of the notice seeking possession and at the date of the hearing of the action, the rent is at least 8 weeks in arrears or two months in arrears.

The discretionary grounds for possession of a property, which is let on an assured tenancy

As we have seen, the discretionary grounds for possession are those in relation to which the court has some powers over whether or not the landlord can evict. In other words, the final decision is left to the judge. Often the judge will prefer to grant a suspended order first, unless the circumstances are dramatic.

Ground Nine applies when suitable alternative accommodation is available or will be when the possession order takes effect. As we have seen, if the landlord wishes to obtain possession of his or her property in order to use it for other purposes then suitable alternative accommodation has to be provided.

Ground Ten deals with rent arrears as does ground eleven. These grounds are distinct from the mandatory grounds, as there does not have to be a fixed arrear in terms of time scale, e.g., 8 weeks. The judge, therefore, has some choice as to whether or not to evict.

Ground Twelve concerns any broken obligation of the tenancy. As we have seen with the protected tenancy, there are a number of conditions of the tenancy agreement, such as the requirement not to racially or sexually harass a neighbor. Ground Twelve will be used if these conditions are broken.

Ground Thirteen deals with the deterioration of the dwelling as a result of a tenant's neglect. This is connected with the structure of the property and is the same as for a protected tenancy. It puts the responsibility on the tenant to look after the premises.

Ground Fourteen concerns nuisance, annoyance and illegal or immoral use. This is where a tenant or anyone connected with the tenant has caused a nuisance to neighbors.

Ground 14A this ground deals with domestic violence.

Ground Fifteen concerns the condition of the furniture and tenants neglect. As Ground thirteen puts some responsibility on the tenant to look after the structure of the building so Ground Fifteen makes the tenant responsible for the furniture and fittings.

The description of the grounds above is intended as a guide only. For a fuller description please refer to the 1988 Housing Act, section 7, Schedule two,) as amended by the 1996 Housing Act) which is available at reference libraries.

THE ASSURED SHORTHOLD TENANCY

An assured shorthold tenancy is the usual form of tenancy used by the private landlord. This is a tenancy granted on or after 15th January 1989 that would have been an assured tenancy but has been granted for a fixed term of at least six months. This is why it is known as a shorthold tenancy. This form of tenancy is very popular with landlords and was, indeed, introduced to weaken tenants security and therefore encourage private landlords to rent out more property.

Any property let on an assured tenancy can be let on an assured shorthold, providing the following three conditions are met:

The tenancy must be for a fixed term of not less than six months.

The agreement cannot contain powers, which enable the landlord to end the tenancy before six months. This does not include the right of the landlord to enforce the grounds for possession, which will be approximately the same as those for the assured tenancy.

A notice must have been served on the tenant before the grant of the tenancy informing him or her that the tenancy is an assured shorthold. A copy of this notice is shown in the Appendix.

A notice requiring possession at the end of the term is usually served two months before that date.

A notice must be served before any rent increase giving one months clear notice and providing details of the rent increase.

As with a protected tenancy or an assured tenancy if the landlord wishes to get possession of his/her property, in this case before the expiry of the contractual term, the landlord has to gain a court order. A notice of seeking possession must be served, giving fourteen days notice and following similar grounds of possession as an assured tenancy.

The landlord cannot simply tell a tenant to leave before the end of the agreed term.

A copy of a notice of seeking possession for an assured shorthold tenancy is shown in the Appendix.

If the tenancy runs on after the end of the fixed term then the landlord can regain possession by giving the required two months notice, as mentioned above.

At the end of the term for which the assured shorthold tenancy has been granted, the landlord has an automatic right to possession.

An assured shorthold tenancy will become periodic (will run from week to week) when the initial term of six months has elapsed and the landlord has not brought the tenancy to an end.

Now read the Key Points from Chapter five.

KEY POINTS

Assured tenancies. All tenancies signed after 15th January 1989, with a few exceptions, are assured tenancies.

Protection. Assured tenancies are not protected and do not have a right to a fair rent.

Security. Assured tenants can only be evicted on certain grounds for possession, after being given a minimum of fourteen days notice and taken to court.

Rents. Assured rents cannot be raised more than once in a one year period.

Fixed term. An assured shorthold tenancy is granted for a minimum period of six months. A notice of assured shorthold tenancy must be received before the tenancy is signed.

6

JOINT TENANCIES AND SUCCESSION TO A TENANCY

JOINT TENANCIES: THE POSITION OF TWO OR MORE PEOPLE WHO HAVE A TENANCY AGREEMENT FOR ONE PROPERTY

Although it is the normal state of affairs for a tenancy agreement, whether secure or assured, to be granted to one person, this is not always the case.

A tenancy can also be granted to two or more people and is then known as a *joint tenancy*. The position of joint tenants is exactly the same as that of single tenants. In other words, there is still one tenancy even though it is shared.

Each tenant is responsible for paying the rent and observing the terms and conditions of the tenancy agreement. No one joint tenant can prevent another joint tenants access to the premises.

If one of the joint tenants dies then his or her interest will automatically pass to the remaining joint tenants. A joint tenant cannot dispose of his or her interest in a will.

If one joint tenant, however, serves a notice to quit (notice to leave the property) on another joint tenant(s) then the tenancy will come to an end and the landlord can apply to court for a possession order, if the remaining tenant does not leave.

The position of a wife or husband in relation to joint tenancies is rather more complex because the married person has more rights when it comes to the home than the single person.

51

Remember: the position of a tenant who has signed a joint tenancy agreement is exactly the same as that of the single tenant. If one person leaves, the other(s) have the responsibilities of the tenancy. If one person leaves without paying his share of the rent then the other tenants will have to pay instead.

SUCCESSION TO A TENANCY IN THE EVENT OF DEATH

Protected tenancies: The right to succeed

As we all know, when a member of the family dies, it can be very distressing. The last thing the family want is for the landlord to be threatening eviction at such a time. It is important for a landlord to know the law in this respect.

When a protected or statutory tenant dies, the landlord is not always entitled to automatic possession of the premises. If the spouse (wife or husband) of the original tenant has lived with him/her prior to his/her death then the spouse is entitled to succeed (take over the tenancy) under law.

If there was no spouse then any other member of the tenants family who lived with the tenant for six months prior to the death can succeed, and becomes a statutory tenant.

If there is a dispute amongst members of the family over who should become the statutory tenant then the matter will be referred to the County Court.

A person who succeeds to a statutory tenancy in this manner can pass the tenancy on, but at the death of the person to whom he/she passed it on the right to succeed ceases.

Succession and assured tenancies

The (legal) right to succeed to an assured tenancy is the same as a protected tenancy subject to a few modifications. A person who was living with the original tenant as husband and wife will be treated as his or her spouse.

It is only the still living former spouse who can succeed to the tenancy. If more than one person was living with the deceased as spouse the court has powers to determine who is entitled. The right to succeed to an assured tenancy is restricted to a person who has lived at the property for more than five years.

Now read the Key Points from Chapter six.

Key Points

Joint tenants. A tenancy granted to two or more people is a joint tenancy. The position of joint tenants is exactly the same as that of a single tenant.

Ending the tenancy. In order to end the tenancy, one of the joint tenants must serve a notice to quit on the other tenant(s).

Succession to a tenancy. If a spouse (wife or husband) or anyone deemed to be a spouse has lived with a protected tenant prior to his/her death then that person may be entitled to succeed to the tenancy.

Other successions. If there was no spouse then any other member of the family resident for six months prior to death can succeed.

Assured tenants right to succeed. An assured tenant also has a right to succeed to a tenancy. A person who was living with the original tenant as husband and wife will be treated as a spouse. It is only the still living former spouse who can succeed to the tenancy.

7

RENT

THE PAYMENT OF RENT AND OTHER FINANCIAL MATTERS

If a tenancy is protected under the Rent Act 1977, as described in Chapter Two, then there is the right to apply to the Rent Officer for the setting of a fair rent for the property.

A fair rent is a rent set by a Rent Officer employed by the Rent Officer Service. The address of this service can be found in the telephone directory. The Rent Officer is based at the offices of the local authority.

Either the landlord or the tenant of a property can apply to register a fair rent. Application is made on a form which is standard and is available from the Rent Officer Service or from a Citizens Advice Bureau.

Once a fair rent has been set it cannot be altered in any way by the landlord.

If a tenancy is assured then the right to a fair rent assessed by a Rent Officer has been removed and the landlord has the right to set a market rent.

This rent will be the equivalent of the rent for a similar property on the open market. If an assured tenant disagrees with the amount charged, he/she can apply to a Rent Assessment Committee for a review. The main principle is that the landlord may not charge more than a market rent.

A landlord can apply only to have a fair rent ended on the basis that the accommodation has ceased to be subject to a protected or statutory tenancy and two years have gone by since the registration of a fair rent.

Application to vary the fair rent can be made at any time by landlord or tenant on the grounds that the circumstances relating to the dwelling have changed thus making the set rent unfair.

THE ASSURED TENANT: THE SITUATION AFTER 1989

The assured tenant has far fewer rights in relation to rent control than the protected tenant.

The Housing Act 1988 allows a landlord to charge whatever he likes. There is no right to a fair or reasonable rent with an assured tenancy. The rent can sometimes be negotiated at the outset of the tenancy. This rent has to be paid as long as the contractual term of the tenancy lasts. Once the contractual term has expired, the landlord is entitled to continue to charge the same rent.

The landlord cannot increase the rent until the tenancy has lasted for at least twelve months. However, a notice of increase may be served in that period. The notice of increase must expire after that twelve month date.

In the case of a yearly tenancy, at least six months notice must be given, or a period of notice equal to the length of the tenancy must be given with a minimum of one month.

The rent increase proposed by the landlord will automatically apply unless it is referred to a Rent Assessment Committee. Reference to the Committee must take place before the notice of proposed increase has been served, otherwise the Committee will have no power to consider it.

Normally the rent decided by the Committee will be backdated to the expiry of the notice unless the tenant can demonstrate undue hardship caused by the backdating.

RENT CONTROL FOR ASSURED SHORTHOLD TENANCIES FOLLOWING THE PASSAGE OF THE 1988 HOUSING ACT

We have seen that the assured shorthold tenancy is for a period of six months minimum. Like the assured tenant, the assured shorthold tenant has no right to request that a fair rent should be set. The rent is a market rent.

As with an assured tenancy, the assured shorthold tenant has the right to appeal to a Rent Assessment Committee in the case of what he/she considers an unreasonable rent. This may be done during the contractual term of the tenancy. The Committee will consider whether the rent is significantly higher than is usual for a similar property.

If the Committee assess a different rent from that set by the landlord, they may set a date when the increase will take effect. The rent cannot be backdated to before the date of the application. Once a decision has been reached by the Committee, the landlord cannot increase the rent for at least twelve months.

COUNCIL TAX AND THE PRIVATE TENANT

From April 1993 the council tax replaced the poll tax. Unlike poll tax, the council tax is based on properties, or dwellings, and not individual people.

This means that there is one bill for each individual dwelling, rather than separate bills for each person. The number and type of people who live in the dwelling may affect the size of the final bill. A discount of 25% is given for people who live alone. Each property is placed in a valuation band with different properties paying more or less depending on their individual value. Tenants who feel that their home has been placed in the wrong valuation band can appeal to their local authority council tax department.

Who has to pay the council tax?

In most cases the tenant occupying the dwelling will have to pay the council tax. However, a landlord will be responsible for paying the council tax where there are several households living in one dwelling. This will usually be hostels, bedsits and other non-self contained flats where people share things such as cooking and washing facilities. The council tax on this type of property remains the responsibility of the landlord even if all but one of the tenants move out.

Although the landlord has the responsibility for paying the council tax, he or she will normally try to pass on the increased cost through rents. However, there is a set procedure for a landlord to follow if he/she wishes to increase rent.

Tenants who moved in before 15th January 1989 without a registered fair rent

A landlord can only increase the rent of these tenants to cover the council tax by giving a correctly worded notice of increase to the tenant or by referring the rent to the Rent Officer for registration.

Tenants with assured tenancies

During the fixed term of the tenancy agreement (usually the first year) the landlord cannot force the tenant to pay a rent increase, not even if this arises from the council tax. Following the fixed term, the landlord may only increase the rent within the rental period by serving a specifically worded notice of increase. The tenant can then either agree the increase or refer it to the Rent Assessment Committee for consideration.

When a notice of increase is given, at least one months notice should be given. If a tenant then refers the notice of increase to the Rent Assessment Committee the increase will be backdated to when the notice was served.

Tenants with assured shorthold tenancies

When the present fixed term of the tenancy comes to an end a landlord can ask for an increase in rent.

Dwellings which are exempt

Certain properties will be exempt from the council tax, such as student's halls of residences and nurses homes. Properties with all students resident will be exempt from the tax. However, if one non-student moves in then that property will no longer be exempt from tax. Uninhabitable empty properties are exempt from tax, as they are not counted as dwellings. This is not the same as homes, which have been declared as unfit for human habitation by Environmental Health officers. The deciding factor will be whether or not a property is capable of being lived in.

Reductions in council tax bills

Tenants in self-contained accommodation who live alone will be entitled to a discount of 25% of the total bill. Tenants may also qualify for the discount if they share their homes with people who do not count for council tax purposes. Such people are: children under eighteen; students; patients resident in hospital; people who are severely mentally impaired; low paid careworkers; eighteen or nineteen year olds still at school (or just left); people in prison (except for non-payment of fines or the council tax); and people caring for someone with a disability who is not a spouse, partner or child under eighteen.

Benefits available for those on low income

Tenants on very low income, except for students, will usually be able to claim council tax benefit. This can cover up to 100% of the council tax.

Tenants with disabilities may be entitled to further discounts. Tenants who are not responsible for individual council tax, but pay it through their rent, can claim housing benefit to cover the increase.

The rules covering council tax liability can be obtained from a Citizens Advice Bureau or from your local authority council tax department.

SERVICE CHARGES

What is a service charge?

A service charge covers provision of services other than those covered by the rent. A rental payment will normally cover maintenance charges, loan charges if any, and also profit. Other services, such as cleaning and gardening, will be covered by a separate charge, known as a service charge. A *registered* rent reflects the cost of any services provided by the landlord. An assured rent set by a landlord will normally include services, which must be outlined in the agreement.

Details of the cost of any services have to be entered on the application form when registering a rent. They must be accompanied by a schedule showing how the figures have been arrived at and the method of apportionment (how they have been shared out) between occupiers if there is more than one tenancy.

The figures can be challenged by the tenant. If the landlord registers a fixed fair rent the part relating to services must be noted separately, unless it is less than 5% of the total rent.

If a service charge is fixed, there is no legal obligation to consult when spending money.

A landlord can also register a *variable* service charge, which means that the cost of services is reset every year, but not less than one year.

The fact that the charges are variable must be written into a tenancy agreement and the landlord has a legal duty to provide the tenant with annual budgets and accounts and has to consult when he or she wishes to spend over a certain amount of money, currently £50 per dwelling or £1,000 per scheme (estate or block of flats), whichever is the greater.

The form of consultation, which must take place, is that of writing to all those affected and informing them of:

The landlords intention to carry out work;

Why these works are seen to be necessary;

The estimated cost of the works;

At least two estimates or the inviting of them to see two estimates.

A period of twenty-eight days must be allowed before work is carried out. This gives time for any feedback from tenants.

The landlord can incur reasonable expense, without consultation, if the work is deemed to be necessary, i.e. emergency works.

If a service charge is variable then a landlord has certain legal obligations which are clearly laid out in the 1985 and 1987 Landlord and Tenant Acts. If you intend to let property for profit then it is of the utmost importance that you understand the law governing service charges.

THE PAYMENT OF PREMIUMS AND DEPOSITS TO A LANDLORD:

It is an offence under the 1977 Rent Act to charge a premium for granting a protected tenancy or, in the case of tenancies with registered rents, for a restricted contract. A *premium* is a payment, a one-off payment.

This is not the case with assured tenancies granted after the Housing Act 1988 came into force. However, if a premium is charged, then it gives the tenant the right to assign the tenancy, i.e., to pass it on to someone else (1988 Housing Act, section 15). Therefore, most private landlords letting property out on an assured shorthold tenancy do not charge a premium.

A landlord can charge a *deposit*, to set against the possibility that a tenant may damage the property or furniture. For most types of tenancy the law puts a limit on the amount that can be charged. The normal amount is 1 months rent.

Now read the Key Points from Chapter seven.

Key Points

Fair rent. If a tenancy is protected under the Rent Act 1977 there will be entitlement to a fair rent set by a Rent Officer.

Increase of fair rent. Once the Rent Officer has set a fair rent the landlord cannot increase it unless he appeals.

Putting the rent up. Even if the fair rent is higher than the existing rent, the landlord cannot charge more until the expiry of the two-year period.

Assured tenancies. If a tenancy is assured there will not be the protection of the 1977 Rent Act and no entitlement to a fair rent. The rent charged would be a market rent.

Appealing a fair rent for protected tenants. If the tenant is not happy with the rent set by the Rent Officer, if a protected tenant, he/she can appeal to a Rent Assessment Committee.

Council tax. If the tenant does not receive an individual bill for council tax then the landlord will be responsible for payment. This is usually the case in a multi-occupied home or block. The landlord cannot increase the rent without either notifying the Rent Officer or giving the required notice if an assured tenant.

Service charge. A service charge is a charge for services such as cleaning or gardening. A landlord must show the cost of services clearly except if the total charge is less than 5% of rent. The service charge can be variable, e.g., varied once a year, or fixed, where it cannot be increased until the end of the two-year period.

Premiums. It is an offence under the 1977 Rent Act to charge a premium for granting a protected tenancy or restricted contract.

Deposits. A landlord can charge a reasonable deposit for a dwelling

After six months. An assured shorthold can be allowed to run on. There is no automatic requirement to renew the agreement. Two months notice of ending the tenancy must be given.

8

THE RIGHT TO QUIET ENJOYMENT OF A HOME

In Chapter three we saw that, when a tenancy agreement is signed, the landlord is contracting to give quiet enjoyment of the tenants home. This means that they have the right to live peacefully in the home without harassment.

The landlord is obliged not to do anything that will disturb the right to the quiet enjoyment of the home. The most serious breach of this right would be for the landlord to wrongfully evict a tenant.

EVICTION: WHAT CAN BE DONE AGAINST UNLAWFUL HARASSMENT AND EVICTION

It is a criminal offence for a landlord unlawfully to evict a residential occupier (whether or not a tenant!). The occupier has protection under the Protection from Eviction Act 1977 section 1(2).

If the tenant or occupier is unlawfully evicted his/her first course should be to seek an injunction compelling the landlord to readmit him/her to the premises.

It is an unfortunate fact but many landlords will attempt to evict tenants forcefully. In doing so they break the law.

However, the landlord may, on termination of the tenancy or licence, recover possession without a court order if the agreement was entered into after 15th January 1989 and it falls into one of the following six situations:

The occupier shares any accommodation with the landlord and the landlord occupies the premises as his or her only or principal home.

The occupier shares any of the accommodation with a member of the landlords family, that person occupies the premises as their only or principal home, and the landlord occupies as his or her only or principal home premises in the same building.

The tenancy or licence was granted temporarily to an occupier who entered the premises as a trespasser.

The tenancy or licence gives the right to occupy for the purposes of a holiday.

The tenancy or licence is rent-free.

The licence relates to occupation of a hostel.

There is also a section in the 1977 Protection from Eviction Act which provides a defense for otherwise unlawful eviction and that is that the landlord may repossess if it is thought that the tenant no longer lives on the premises.

It is important to note that, in order for such action to be seen as a crime under the 1977 Protection from Eviction Act, the intention of the landlord to evict must be proved.

However, there is another offence, namely harassment, which also needs to be proved. Even if the landlord is not guilty of permanently depriving a tenant of their home he/she could be guilty of harassment.

Such actions as cutting off services, deliberately allowing the premises to fall into a state of disrepair, or even forcing unwanted sexual attentions, all constitute harassment and a breach of the right to *quiet enjoyment.*

The 1977 Protection from Eviction Act also prohibits the use of violence to gain entry to premises. Even in situations where the landlord has the right to gain entry without a court order it is an offence to use violence.

If entry to the premises is opposed then the landlord should gain a court order.

What can be done against unlawful evictions

There are two main remedies for unlawful eviction: damages and, as stated above, an injunction.

The injunction

An injunction is an order from the court requiring a person to do, or not to do something. In the case of eviction the court can grant an injunction requiring the landlord to allow a tenant back into occupation of the premises. In the case of harassment an order can be made preventing the landlord from harassing the tenant.

Failure to comply with an injunction is contempt of court and can result in a fine or imprisonment.

Damages

In some cases the tenant can press for *financial compensation* following unlawful eviction. Financial compensation may have to be paid in cases where financial loss has occurred or in cases where personal hardship alone has occurred.

The tenant can also press for *special damages*, which means that the tenant may recover the definable out-of-pocket expenses. These could be expenses arising as a result of having to stay in a hotel because of the eviction. Receipts must be kept in that case. There are also *general damages*, which can be awarded in compensation for stress, suffering and inconvenience.

A tenant may also seek *exemplary damages* where it can be proved that the landlord has disregarded the law deliberately with the intention of making a profit out of the displacement of the tenant.

Now read the Key Points from Chapter eight.

KEY POINTS

Quiet enjoyment. A tenant has the right to quiet enjoyment of his/her home.

Eviction. It is a criminal offence to unlawfully evict a tenant from his or her home.

Use of force. There are certain circumstances in which the landlord can recover possession without a court order but he/she cannot use force to evict a tenant.

Tenants rights. If a tenant is unlawfully evicted, he/she can seek an injunction to force the landlord to let them back into their home. They can also seek damages for harassment and inconvenience.

9

REPAIRS AND IMPROVEMENTS:

REPAIRS AND IMPROVEMENTS GENERALLY

THIS CHAPTER SETS OUT THE OBLIGATIONS THAT THE LANDLORD HAS WITH REGARD TO REPAIRS AND IMPROVEMENTS WITHIN A TENANTED PROPERTY

Repairs are essential works to keep the property in good order. Improvements are alterations to the property, e.g. the installation of a shower.

As we have seen, most tenancies are periodic, i.e. week to week or month to month. If a tenancy falls into this category, or is a fixed-term tenancy for less than seven years, and began after October 1961, then a landlord is legally responsible for most major repairs to the flat or house.

If a tenancy began after 15th January 1989 then, in addition to the above responsibility, the landlord is also responsible for repairs to common parts and service fittings.

The area of law dealing with the landlord and tenants repairing obligations is the 1985 Landlord and Tenant Act, section 11.

This section of the Act is known as a covenant and cannot be excluded by informal agreement between landlord and tenant. In other words the landlord is legally responsible whether he or she likes it or not. Parties to a tenancy, however, may make an application to a court mutually to vary or exclude this section.

An example of repairs a landlord is responsible for:

Leaking roofs and guttering;

Rotting windows;

Rising damp;

Damp walls;

Faulty electrical wiring;

Dangerous ceilings and staircases;

Faulty gas and water pipes;

Broken water heaters and boilers;

Broken lavatories, sinks or baths.

In shared housing the landlord must see that shared halls, stairways, kitchens and bathrooms are maintained and kept clean and lit.

Normally, tenants are responsible only for minor repairs, e.g., broken door handles, cupboard doors, etc. Tenants will also be responsible for decorations unless they have been damaged as a result of the landlord's failure to do repair.

A landlord will be responsible for repairs only if the repair has been reported. It is therefore important to report repairs in writing and keep a copy. If the repair is not carried out then action can be taken. Damages can also be claimed.

Compensation can be claimed, with the appropriate amount being the reduction in the value of the premises to the tenant caused by the landlord's failure to repair. If the tenant carries out the repairs then the amount expended will represent the decrease in value.

The tenant does not have the right to withhold rent because of a breach of repairing covenant by the landlord. However, depending on the repair, the landlord will not have a very strong case in court if rent is withheld.

REPORTING REPAIRS TO A LANDLORD

The tenant has to tell the landlord or the person collecting the rent straight away when a repair needs doing. It is advisable that it is in writing, listing the repairs that need to be done.

Once a tenant has reported a repair the landlord must do it within a reasonable period of time. What is reasonable will depend on the nature of the repair.

If certain emergency work needs to be done, such as leaking guttering or drains a quick notice can be served ordering the landlord to do the work within a short time. In exceptional cases if a home cannot be made habitable at reasonable cost the council may declare that the house must no longer be used, in which case the council has a legal duty to rehouse a tenant.

If after the council has served notice the landlord still does not do the work, the council can send in its own builder or, in some cases take the landlord to court. A tenant must allow a landlord access to do repairs. The landlord has to give twenty four hours notice of wishing to gain access.

The tenants rights whilst repairs are being carried out

The landlord must ensure that the repairs are done in an orderly and efficient way with minimum inconvenience to the tenant If the works are disruptive or if property or decorations are damaged the tenant can apply to the court for compensation or, if necessary, for an order to make the landlord behave reasonably.

If the landlord genuinely needs the house empty to do the work he/she can ask the tenant to vacate it and can if necessary get a court order against the tenant.

A *written agreement* should be drawn up making it clear that the tenant can move back in when the repairs are completed and stating what the arrangements for fuel charges and rent are.

If a person is an *assured* tenant the landlord could get a court order to

71

make that person give up the home permanently if there is work to be done with him/her in occupation in occupation.

Can the landlord put the rent up after doing repairs?

If there is a service charge for maintenance, the landlord may be able to pass on the cost of the work(s). A registered rent cannot be increased until the registration period has expired. The rent officer will take into account the repairs carried out. The landlord can have the rent reassessed before expiry only if major works or improvements have been carried out.

Tenants rights to make improvements to a property

Unlike repairs you will not normally have the right to insist that the landlord make actual alterations to the home. However, a tenant needs the following amenities and the law states that you should have them:

Bath or shower;

Wash hand basin;

Hot and cold water at each bath, basin or shower;

An indoor toilet.

If these amenities do not exist then the tenant can contact the council's Environmental Health Officer. An improvement notice can be served on the landlord ordering him to put the amenity in.

DISABLED TENANTS: RIGHTS AND OBLIGATIONS

If a tenant is disabled he/she may need special items of equipment in the accommodation. The local authority may help in providing and, occasionally, paying for these. You will need to obtain the permission from the landlord. If you require more information then contact the social services department locally.

SHARED HOUSING: THE POSITION OF TENANTS IN A SHARED HOUSE

The law lays down special standards for shared housing (houses in multiple occupation). Local authorities have special powers to deal with bad conditions when they occur. The legal regulations for houses in multiple occupation are set out in the Housing (Management of Houses in Multiple Occupation) Regulations 1990 and also the Housing Act 1996.

The manager of a house in multiple occupation has responsibilities under the management regulations to carry out repair, maintenance and cleaning work and also safety work necessary to protect residents from risk of injury. A notice must be displayed where all the residents can see it showing the name, address and telephone number of the manager. Landlords must ensure that main entrances shared passageways, staircases and other common areas are maintained. All services such as gas, electricity and water supplies, plus drainage facilities, must also be maintained.

The same rules apply to the internal areas of living accommodation. In addition, there is a duty to maintain adequate fire safety, as obviously, shared housing is at greater risk of fire. Self-closing fire doors, emergency escape lighting, fire alarms and detectors and fire fighting equipment will normally be required. Signs indicating fire escape routes must be displayed where they are easy to see.

There are also rules concerning overcrowding in shared housing. The local authority has powers to tackle overcrowding problems; landlords, on request, have to supply the local authority with numbers of individuals and households in a shared house. Tenants also have duties, which enable landlords to fulfil their legal responsibilities. Tenants should allow landlords access at reasonable times, give details of all who live in the accommodation, and take care to avoid damage to property.

SANITATION: HEALTH AND HYGIENE

Local authorities have a duty to serve an owner with a notice requiring the provision of WCs when a property has insufficient sanitation, sanitation meaning toilet waste disposal.

They will also serve notice if it is thought that the existing sanitation is inadequate and is harmful to health or is a nuisance.

Local authorities have similar powers under various Public Health Acts to require owners to put right bad drains and sewers, also food storage facilities and vermin, plus the containing of disease.

The Environmental Health Department, if it considers the problem bad enough will serve a notice requiring the landlord to put the defect right. In certain cases the local authority can actually do the work and require the landlord to pay for it. This is called work *in default.*

RENOVATION GRANTS: A TENANTS RIGHT TO A GRANT TO CARRY OUT WORK ON THE PROPERTY IF A PRIVATE TENANT

In certain cases the local authority will give assistance towards essential works on properties. Usually it is a part *grant* and is *means tested*; i.e. the amount you get depends on your income.

There are different kinds of help to suit different needs, depending on the type of property involved and the scale of the work you may want to carry out.

Grants may be available towards the cost of repairs, improvements, and conversions of buildings and of providing facilities and adaptations for disabled people. In addition, minor assistance may also be available to help some tenants who want to carry out small-scale work on their homes.

There are certain circumstances where a tenant, can apply for a grant. In a lot of cases a landlord would apply because it is his/her property.

The types of work which attract grant are as follows:

Renovation grant

The main purpose for which renovation grant is intended is to bring a property up to the standard of fitness for human habitation: this includes bringing properties back up to a certain standard. Therefore typical work would be home insulation and for heating, for providing satisfactory internal arrangements and for conversions (of old houses).

The amount of grant available will be determined by the central and local government policy then in force and will almost certainly be means-tested.

Common parts grant

There is another form of grant available, the common parts grant which is applicable to blocks of flats, or houses converted into flats. Both landlord and tenant together can apply for this type of grant. Occupying tenants can apply for this grant together, without the landlord, provided that they are all liable under the terms of the tenancy agreement. Again, this grant is means-tested and is a partial grant.

There are other forms of grant available but in the main only a landlord would apply for them, such as a houses in multiple occupation grant.

In this book, there is space only or the briefest of outlines concerning the availability of grants. The first point of enquiry in relation to grants should be your local authority, which can advise you further.

Now read the Key Points from Chapter nine.

Key Points

Responsibility for repairs. If a tenancy is periodic or of a fixed term for less than seven years and began after October 1961, a landlord is legally responsible for certain repairs.

The law. The landlord has repairing obligations under the Landlord and Tenant Act 1985, section 11.

Tenants responsibility. Normally, tenants are responsible only for minor internal repairs.

Landlords responsibility. A landlord will only be responsible for a repair if it has been reported.

Local authority. If a landlord does not carry out repairs then the local authority in particular the Environmental Health Department can get involved.

Inconvenience. A tenant has certain rights whilst repairs are being done, particularly for inconvenience.

Improvements. A tenant will not normally have the right to make improvements. However, they are entitled to certain basic amenities, such as a shower or a bath.

Disabled. A disabled tenant may need certain items of equipment in their home. The local authority can advise and assist in this area, even helping with payment.

Shared housing. There are special laws governing housing in multiple occupation (shared housing) particularly in relation to health and safety. The local authority can advise.

Local authority grants. Private tenants may be entitled to a grant to help with work on a property. The local authority will advise on entitlement.

10

THE LANDLORD AND INCOME TAX
THE LANDLORD AND HOUSING BENEFIT

Rent received by a landlord is treated as income for tax purposes. The basis upon which tax is assessed is to some extent dependent on whether or not the property is furnished or unfurnished. However, these differences in taxation are unlikely to have any affect on the way that the small landlord is taxed. Agents who receive rent on a landlord's behalf can be required to pay a proportion to the Inland Revenue on account of the tax liability. This arrangement will largely depend on the landlords previous tax history. If such a direction is made then the agent must comply. If the tenant lives abroad then the tenant is under a legal obligation to deduct basic rate income tax from the rent and pay it to the Inland Revenue.

Exemptions from tax

Where the landlord lets rooms in his own home a certain amount of rent, currently £3250 per annum is exempt from tax. If there is more than one landlord, such as a couple who share the home this allowance is split between them. They cannot both claim the allowance.

Deductions from tax

Expenditure from the property can be deducted from the rental income to arrive at a final figure on which tax must be paid. The following are all deductible:

• Insuring the property

- Repairs and maintenance
- Agents fees or commission
- Water rates
- Council tax
- Any rent paid to a superior landlord, such a crevice charges etc.
- Legal fees
- Interest paid on loans secured on the property, i.e., mortgages, although there are exceptions to this.

Improvements, as opposed to repairs, carried out on the property are not deductible. In practice, unless an enormous allowance is claimed, the Inland Revenue are not likely to enquire too much about this.

Payment of housing benefit directly to the landlord

Housing benefit is a payment made to the tenant rather than the landlord. The Amount of benefit that a tenant is paid will very much depend on that person circumstances. The rules regarding payment of housing benefit have tightened considerably over the years and if you know that a tenant is going to be claiming housing b benefit then you should be sure that they will be entitled. Local authorities have local rents that they will pay and they will not pay, for example, for a single person to occupy a accommodation surplus to their needs or for anyone to claim what they see as excessive rent.

It is possible to arrange for the local authority to pay housing benefit direct to the landlord, especially where there are more than eight weeks in arrears. If there is an arrears problem and the landlord believes that the tenant is entitled to, or may be receiving housing benefit then the local authority should be contacted.

Housing benefit and possession for arrears of rent

Very often, problems in obtaining benefit will cause tenants to accrue rent arrears. If a landlord has let a property knowing that the tenant is claiming housing benefit it is better to wait for the tenant to sort it out. The court is unlikely to give possession if arrears are accruing because of benefit. Once there are eight weeks of arrears (see grounds for possession) then the court has no choice but to give possession anyway and quite often it is better to wait rather than jumping the gun and losing rental income altogether.

If on the other hand the tenant has stated that they are going to pay rent personally rather than benefit then the court will look more favorably on-giving possession to the landlord if arrears have arisen as a result of an immediate claim for benefit.

11

What should be provided under the tenancy

Furniture

A landlords decision whether or not to furnish property will depend on the sort of tenant that he is aiming to find. The actual legal distinction between a furnished property and an unfurnished property has faded into insignificance.

If a landlord does let a property as furnished then the following would be the absolute minimum:

- Seating, such as sofa and armchair

- Cabinet or sideboard

- Kitchen tables and chairs

- Cooker and refrigerator

- Bedroom furniture

Even unfurnished lets, however, are expected to come complete with a basic standard of furniture, particularly carpets and kitchen goods. If the landlord does supply electrical equipment then he or she is able to disclaim any repairing responsibility for it, but this must be mentioned in the tenancy agreement.

Services

Usually, a landlord will only provide services to a tenant if the property is a flat situated in a block or is a house on a private estate. The services will usually include cyclical painting and maintenance, usually on a three to four year basis (flats) and gardening and cleaning plus repairs to the communal areas, plus communal electricity bills and water rates. These services should be outlined in the agreement and are administered within a strict framework of law, The 1985 Landlord and Tenant Act Section 18-30 as amended by the 1987 LTA. The landlord has rigid duties imposed within this Act, such as the need to gain estimates before commencing works and also to consult with residents where the cost exceeds £50 per flat or £1000 whichever is the greater. The landlord must give the tenant 28 days notice of works inviting feedback

Tenants have the right to see audited accounts and invoices relating to work. Service charges, as an extra payment over and above the rent are always contentious and it is an area that Landlords need to be aware of if they are to manage professionally.

Repairs

See chapter on repairing obligations

Insurance

Strictly speaking, there is no duty on either landlord or tenant to insure the property. However, it is highly advisable for the landlord to provide buildings insurance as he/she stands to lose a lot more in the event of fire or other disaster than the tenant. A landlord letting property for a first time would be well advised to consult his/ her insurance company before letting as there are different criteria to observe when a property is let and not to inform the company could invalidate the policy.

At the end of the tenancy

The tenancy agreement will normally spell out the obligations of the tenant at the end of the term. Essentially, the tenant will have an obligation to:

- have kept the interior clean and tidy and in a good state of repair and decoration

- have not caused any damage

- have replaced anything that they have broken

- replace or pay for the repair of anything that they have damaged

- pay for the laundering of the linen

- pay for any other laundering

- put anything that they have moved or removed back to how it was

Sometimes a tenancy agreement will include for the tenants paying for anything that is soiled at their own expense, although sensible wear and tear is allowed for.

The landlord will normally be able to recover any loss from the deposit that the tenant has given on entering the premises. However, sometimes, the tenements will withhold rent for the last month in order to recoup their deposit. It is up to the landlord to negotiate re-imbursement for any damage caused, but this should be within reason. There is a remedy, which can be pursued in the Small Claims court if the tenants refuse to pay but this is rarely successful.

12

GOING TO COURT TO REGAIN POSSESSION OF YOUR PROPERTY

There may come a time when you need to go to court to regain possession of your property. This will usually arise when the contract has been breached by the tenant, for non payment of rent or for some other breach such as nuisance or harassment.

Any move to regain your property for breach of agreement will commence in the county court in the area in which the property is. The first steps in ending the tenancy will necessitate the serving of a notice of seeking possession using one of the Grounds for Possession detailed earlier in the book. If the tenancy is protected then 28 days must be given, the notice must be in prescribed form and served on the tenant personally (preferably).

If the tenancy is assured, which is more often the case now, then 14 days notice of seeking possession can be used. In all cases the ground to be relied upon must be clearly outlined in the notice.

If the case is more complex, then this will entail a particulars of claim being prepared, usually by a solicitor, as opposed to a standard possession form.

A fee is paid when sending the particulars to court, which is currently £80. The standard form which the landlord uses for routine rent arrears cases is called the N119 (see appendix) and the accompanying summons is called the N5. Both of these forms can be obtained from the court. When completed, the forms should be sent in duplicate to the county court and a copy retained for yourself.

The court will send a copy of the Particulars of claim and the summons to the tenant. They will send you a "Plaint note" which gives you a case number and court date to appear, known as the return date.

On the return date, you should arrive at court at least 15 minutes early. You can represent yourself in simple cases but are advised to use a solicitor for more contentious cases.

When it is your turn to present the case, you should have your file in order, a copy of all relevant notices served and a current rent arrears figure or a copy of the particulars for other cases. If it is simple rent arrears then quite often the judge will guide you through. However, the following are the steps to observe:

State your name and address
Tenants name and address
Start date of tenancy
Current rent and arrears
Date notice served-a copy should be produced for the judge
Circumstances of tenant (financial and other) this is where you make
Your case
Copy of order wanted

If the tenant is present then they will have a chance to defend themselves.

A number of orders are available. However, if you have gone to court on the mandatory ground eight then if the fact is proved then you will get possession immediately. If not, then the judge can grant an order, suspended whilst the tenant finds time to pay.

In a lot of cases, it is more expedient for a landlord to serve notice requiring possession, if the tenancy has reached the end of the period, and then wait two months before the property is regained. This saves the cost and time of going to court particularly if the ground is one of nuisance or other which will involve solicitors.

In many cases, if you are contemplating going to court and have never been before and do not know the procedure then it is best to use a solicitor to guide the case through. Costs can be recovered from the tenant, although this depends on the tenants means.

If you regain possession of your property midway through the contractual term then you will have to complete the possession process by use of bailiff, a fee of £80 and another form, Warrant for Possession of Land used.

If you have reached the end of the contractual term and wish to recover your property then a "fast track" procedure is available which entails gaining an order for possession and bailiffs order by post. This can be used in cases with the exception of rent arrears.

GLOSSARY

A SUMMARY OF IMPORTANT TERMS

FREEHOLDER: Someone who owns their property outright.

LEASEHOLDER: Someone who has been granted permission to live on someone else's land for a fixed term.

TENANCY: One form of lease, the most common types of which are fixed-term or periodic.

LANDLORD: A person who owns the property in which the tenant lives.

LICENCE: A licence is an agreement entered into whereby the landlord is merely giving you permission to occupy his/her property for a limited period of time.

TRESPASSER: Someone who has no right through an agreement to live in a property.

PROTECTED TENANT: In the main, subject to certain exclusions, someone whose tenancy began before 15th January 1989.

ASSURED TENANT: In the main, subject to certain exclusions, someone whose tenancy began after 15th January 1989.

STATUTORY TENANT: A person whose original tenancy (contractual term) has been brought to an end by notice or otherwise but not by a court of law.

NOTICE TO QUIT: A legal document giving the protected tenant twenty eight days notice that the landlord intends to apply for possession of the property to the County Court.

GROUND FOR POSSESSION: One of the stated reasons for which the landlord can apply for possession of the property.

MANDATORY GROUND: Where the judge must give possession of the property.

DISCRETIONARY GROUND: Where the judge may or may not give possession, depending on his own opinion.

RESTRICTED CONTRACT: Where the landlord of a pre-1989 tenancy lived on the premises at the time of commencement of the tenancy.

STUDENT LETTING: A tenancy granted by a specified educational institution.

HOLIDAY LETTING: A dwelling used for holiday purposes only.

AGRICULTURAL HOLDING: A dwelling occupied by a person responsible for the control of farming on a holding.

PROTECTED SHORTHOLD TENANCY: A fixed-term pre-1989 tenancy.

ASSURED SHORTHOLD TENANCY: A fixed-term post-1989 tenancy.

SUCCESSION TO A TENANCY: Where the person living with a tenant, either protected or assured, may be entitled, either by way of law or by contract, to succeed to that tenancy on the death of the tenant.

PAYMENT OF RENT: Where you pay a regular sum of money in return for permission to occupy a property or land for a specified period of time.

FAIR RENT: A rent set by the Rent Officer every two years for most pre-1989 tenancies and which is lower than a market rent.

MARKET RENT: A rent deemed to be comparable with other non-fair rents in the area.

RENT ASSESSMENT COMMITTEE: A committee set up to review rents set by either the Rent Officer or the landlord.

PREMIUM: A sum of money charged for permission to live in a property.

DEPOSIT: A sum of money held against the possibility of damage to property.

QUIET ENJOYMENT: The right to live peacefully in your own home.

REPAIRS: Work required to keep a property in good order.

IMPROVEMENTS: Alterations to a property.

LEGAL AID: Help with your legal costs which is dependent on income.

HOUSING BENEFIT: Financial help with rent, which is dependent on income.

HOUSING ADVICE CENTRE: A center which exists to give advice on housing-related matters and which is usually local authority-funded.

LAW CENTRE: A center, which exists for the purpose of assisting the public with legal advice.

INDEX

APPENDIX

1. TYPICAL RESIDENTIAL TENANCY AGREEMENT

2. NOTICE SEEKING POSSESSION OF A PROPERTY LET ON ASSURED TENANCY

3. NOTICE REQUIRING POSSESSION OF AN ASSURED SHORTHOLD TENANCY

4. NOTICE TO QUIT

APPENDIX 1

TYPICAL RESIDENTIAL TENANCY AGREEMENT

Type of Agreement

(ie Assured - Protected)

This tenancy agreement is made on the _____ between
_____ (the Landlord) of _____
_____ (address) and _____ (the Tenant).

It is as agreed as follows:

ADDRESS   1. In respect of _____
_____
_____

DATE AND   2. The Tenancy begins on the _____ day of _____
START OF   19___ for a term of _____ (periodic or fixed)
TENANCY   subject to the terms contained in this Agreement.

RENT   3. The rent due for the premises is as follows:-

Rent	£
Water Rates	£
Service Charge	£
Other Charge	£_____
TOTAL	£_____

Rent is payable weekly in advance, the first payment to be
made on the _____ day of _____ 19___

RENT   4. Details of proposed rent review dates.
REVIEW

CONDITIONS   5. This tenancy is subject to the terms set out in this

| OF TENANCY | Tenancy Agreement and the attached Conditions of Tenancy which you should read very carefully. |

OF TENANCY — Tenancy Agreement and the attached Conditions of Tenancy which you should read very carefully.

TYPE OF AGREEMENT — 6. Details concerning type of agreement.

VARIATION OF TERMS — 7. The Landlord may vary the terms of this Agreement by giving the Tenant 4 weeks' notice of such changes, such a Notice being validly served if sent to the Tenant at the property.

SERVICE OF NOTICES — 8. Any notice including notices in proceedings or written request or consent required to be sent in respect of the Tenancy shall be deemed to have been served on the Tenant if addressed to that Tenant and delivered by hand or sent by post to the Property or to the Tenant's last known address. Any notice including notices in proceedings or written requests to be served on the Landlord shall be deemed to be served if addressed.

I have read this Agreement and the attached Conditions and I accept the tenancy on these terms.

SIGNED BY THE TENANT   _____

DATE   _____

TIME   _____

In the presence of:

NAME   _____

ADDRESS   _____

    _____

OCCUPATION   _____

SIGNATURE   _____

CONDITIONS OF TENANCY

The Landlord Agrees:-

POSSESSION

1. To give the Tenant possession of the Premises at the commencement of the Tenancy.

TENANTS RIGHT
TO OCCUPY

2. Not to interrupt or interfere with the Tenant's right peacefully to occupy the Premises except where -
(i) access is required to inspect the conditions of the Premises or to carry out repairs or other works to the Premises or adjoining property: (The Landlord will normally give at least 24 hours' notice but immediate access may be required in an emergency)
or (ii) a court has given the Landlord possession after the Tenancy has come to an end.

RATES AND
OTHER CHARGES

3. To pay to the respective Local Authority and Water Authority any amounts due to them and collected from the Tenant by way of rates and any other charges. This will not apply when the Tenant is responsible for making payment direct to the authorities.

REPAIR OF
STRUCTURE
AND EXTERIOR

4. To repair the structure and exterior of the premises to a wind and weathertight condition including:-

(i) drains, gutters and external pipes;
(ii) the roof;
(iii) outside walls, outside doors, window sills, window catches, sash cords and window frames;
(iv) internal walls, floors and ceilings, doors and door frames, door hinges and skirting boards;
(v) chimneys, chimney stacks and flues but not including sweeping;
(vi) pathways, steps or other means of access;
(vii) plasterwork.

| REPAIR OF INSTALLATIONS | 5. | To keep in good repair and working order any installations provided by the Landlord for space heating, water heating and sanitation and for the supply of water, gas and electricity, including - |

(i) basins, sinks, baths, toilets, flushing systems and waste pipes;
(ii) electric wiring including sockets and switches, gas pipes and water pipes;
(iii) water heaters, fireplaces, fitted fires and central heating installations.

THE TENANTS OBLIGATIONS

The Tenant Agrees:-

| POSSESSION | 1. | To take possession of the Premises at the commencement of the Tenancy and not to part with possession of the Premises, sub-let the whole or any part of it or take in lodgers or to leave the Premises vacant for more than 4 weeks (without prior arrangement with the Landlord. |

| RENT | 2. | To pay the rent and other charges weekly in advance. |

| USE OF PREMISES | 3. | To use the Premises for residential purposes only. |

| NUISANCE | 4. | Not to cause or allow members of his/her household or invited visitors to cause a nuisance or annoyance to neighbours'or other Tenants of the Landlord. |

| HARASSMENT | 5. | (i) Not to commit or allow to be commited by members of his/her household or visitor any form of racial harassment which may interfere with the peace and the comfort of, or cause offence to, any other tenant, member of his/her household, visitors, neighbours or employee of the Landlord. |

(ii) Not to commit or allow to be commited by members of his/her household or visitors any form of harassment on the grounds of religion, sex, sexual orientation or disability, which may interfere with the peace and comfort of, or cause offence to, any other tenant, member of his/her household, visitors, neighbours or employee of the Landlord.

NOISE 6. Not to permit any radio, television or musical instrument to be played in such a manner to cause a nuisance or an annoyance to neighbours or so as to be audible outside the property between 11.00pm and 7.30am.

PETS 7. (i) To obtain the written consent of the Landlord before keeping a dog or other animals or birds in the Property (including the garden) which might cause a nuisance to the neighbours.

(ii) Not to keep livestock in the Property (including any garden provided).

DAMAGE 8. To make good any damage to the Premises or the furniture, fixtures and fittings or to the common parts caused by the Tenant or any members of the Tenant's household or any invited visitor to the Premises, fair wear and tear expected, and to pay any costs incurred by the Landlord carrying out such works in default.

REPORTING DISREPAIR 9. To report to the Landlord promptly any disrepair or defect for which the Landlord is responsible in the structure or exterior of the Premises or in any installation therein or in the common parts.

ACCESS 10. To allow the Landlord's employees or contractors acting on behalf of the Landlord access during all reasonable hours of the daytime to inspect the condition of the Premises or to carry out repairs or other works to the Premises or adjoining Property. (The Landlord will normally give at least 24 hours' notice but immediate access may be required in an emergency).

Ending the Tenancy

BY THE TENANT
1. The Tenant may end the Tenancy by giving the Landlord at least 4 weeks' notice in writing.

BY THE LANDLORD
2. The Landlord will take steps to bring the Tenancy to an end if the Tenant has broken or failed to perform any of the conditions of this tenancy. In that case a Notice of Quit/Seeking Possession will be served on the Tenant giving 28 days' notice of Court proceedings depending on the reason that the Landlord has for taking proceedings.

OBTAINING POSSESSION
3. Following the expiry of the Notice to Quit or the Notice Requiring Possession, the Landlord will apply to the Court for possession.

MOVING OUT
4. The Tenant will give the Landlord vacant possession and return the keys to the Premises at the end of the Tenancy and remove all personal possessions and rubbish and leave the Premises and the Landlords furniture, fixtures and fittings in good lettable condition and repair. The Landlord accepts no responsibility for anything left at the Premises by the Tenant at the end of the Tenancy.

PREMISES
5. If the premises are left unoccupied by the Tenant for a period of more than 4 weeks the Landlord may assume that the Premises have been abandoned and will then serve a Notice terminating the Tenancy unless the Tenant has previously advised the Landlord of his/her intended temporary absence and has made arrangements for the payment of rent due in that period.

* Whichever grounds are set out in paragraph 3 the court may allow the other grounds to be added to at a later date. If this is done, you will be told about it so you can discuss the additional grounds at the court hearing as well as the grounds set out in paragraph 3.

4. Particulars of each ground are as follows -
Give a full explanation of why each ground is being relied on. (Continue on a separate sheet if necessary.)

_____

* If the court is satisfied that any of grounds 1 to 8 is established it must make an order (but see below in respect of fixed term tendancies).

* Before the court will grant an order on any grounds 9 to 16, it must be satisfied that it I reasonable to require you to lease. This means that, if one of these grounds is set out in paragraph 3, you will be able to suggest to the court that it is not reasonable that you should have to leave, even if you accept that the ground applies.

* The court will not make an order under grounds 1, 3 to 7, 9 or 16, to take effect during the fixed term of the tenancy; and it will only make an order during the fixed term on grounds 2, 8 or 10 to 15 if the terms of the tenancy make provision for it to be brought to an end on any of these grounds.

* Where the court proceedings will not begin until after_____ 19_____
Give the date after which the court proceedings can be brought.

* Where the Landlord is seeking possession under grounds 1, 2, 5 to 7, 9 or 16 in Schedule 2, court proceedings cannot begin earlier than 2 months from the date this notice is served on you and not before the date on which the tenancy (had it not been assured) could have been brought to an end by a notice to quit served at the same time as this notice.

* Where the Landlord is seeking possession on grounds 3, 4, 8 or 10 to 15, court proceedings cannot begin until two weeks after the date this notice is served.

* After the date shown in paragraph 5, court proceedings may be begun at once but not later than 12 months from the date the notice is served. After this

time the notice will lapse and a new notice must be served before possession can be sought.

To be signed by the Landlord or his agent (someone acting for him).

Signed_____   If signed by agent, name and address
Name(s) of_____   of agent
Landlord(s)_____   _____
Address of_____   _____
Landlord(s)_____   _____
Tel: _____   Tel: _____
Date: _____ 19_____   Date: _____ 19_____

NOTICE SEEKING POSSESSION OF A
PROPERTY LET ON AN ASSURED TENANCY

* Please Write Clearly in Black Ink.

* Do not use this form if possession is sought from an assured shorthold tenant under section 21 of the Housing Act 1988 or if the property is occupied under an assured agricultural occupancy.

* This notice is the first step towards requiring you to give up possession of your home. You should read it very carefully.

* If you need advice about this notice, and what you think you should do about it, take it as quickly as possible to any of the following:-

- a Citizens' Advice Bureau
- a Housing Aid Centre
- a Law Centre
- or a Solicitor

You may be able to get Legal Aid but this will depend on your personal circumstances.

1. To:_____ *Name(s) of tenant(s)*

Your Landlord intends to apply to the court for an order requiring you to give up possession of

_____
_____ *Address of Premises*

* If you have an assured tenancy under the Housing Act 1988, which is not an assured shorthold tenancy, you can only be required to leave your home if your Landlord gets an order for possession from the Court on one of the grounds which are set out in Schedule 2 to the Act.

* If you are willing to give up possession of your home without a court order, you should tell the person who signed this notice as soon as possible ad say when you can leave.

3. The Landlord intends to seek possession on the ground(s) _____ in Schedule 2 to the Housing Act 1988, which reads:-
Give the full text of each ground which is being relied on. (Continue on a separate sheet is necessary.) _____

NOTICE REQUIRING POSSESSION OF AN
ASSURED SHORTHOLD TENANCY
(Housing Act 1988 Section 21 (1) (b))

To: _____

Of: _____

We (the landlord(s)) hereby give you notice that we require possession of the dwelling house known as _____
on _____ or at the end of the period of you tenancy which will end next after a period of two calendar months from the service upon you of this Notice.

Dated _____

Signed _____

PRESCRIBED INFORMATION

1.   If the tenant or licensee does not leave the dwelling, the landlord or licensor must get an order for possession from the Court before the tenant or licensee can lawfully be evicted. The landlord or licensor cannot apply for such an order before the Notice to Determine has run out.

2.   A tenant or licensee who does not know if he has any right to remain in possession after a Notice to Quit or a Notice to Determine runs out can obtain advice from a solicitor. Help with all or part of the cost of legal advice and assistance may be available from the Legal Aid Scheme. He should also be able to obtain Information from a Citizen's Advice Bureau, a Housing Aid Centre or a Rent Officer.

NOTES FOR TENANT

1.   On or after the coming to an end of a fixed term Assured Shorthold Tenancy, a court must make an order for possession if the landlord has given notice in this form.

2.   The length of the notice must be at least two calendar months, and the notice must be given before or on the day on which the fixed term comes to an end.

NOTICE TO QUIT ADDRESSED TO A TENANT

NOTICE TO QUIT

To_____

We (name of the agent giving notice) on behalf of your Landlord(s)

_____of_____give you

notice to quit and deliver up possession to him of _____

on_____or the day on which a complete period of your tenancy expires next after the end of four weeks from the service of this notice.

Date_____

Signed (Solicitor or other agent)_____
The name and address of the agent who served this notice is

_____

Information for tenant

1. If the Tenant of licensee does not leave the dwelling, the Landlord or licensor must get an order for possession from the court before the Tenant of licensee can lawfully be evicted. The Landlord or licensor cannot apply for such an order before the notice to quit or notice to determine has run out.

2. A Tenant or Licensee who does not know if he has any right to remain in possession after a notice to determine runs out can obtain advice from a solicitor. Help with all part of the cost of legal advice and the assistance may be available under the Legal Aid Scheme. He should also be able to obtain information from a Citizens' Advice Bureau, a Housing Aid Centre or a Rent Officer.

Notes

1. Notice to quit any premises let as a dwelling must be given at least 4 weeks before it takes effect and it must be in writing (Protection from Eviction Act 1977, section 5)

2. Where a notice to quit is given by a Landlord to determine a tenancy of any premises let as a dwelling, the notice must contain this information